The Havocs

JACOB POLLEY was born in Carlisle in 1975.
He is the author of two poetry collections, both
published by Picador, and a novel, *Talk of the Town*.
He teaches at the University of St Andrews
and lives in Fife.

Jacob Polley

The Havocs

PICADOR

First published 2012 by Picador
an imprint of Pan Macmillan, a division of Macmillan Publishers Limited
Pan Macmillan, 20 New Wharf Road, London N1 9RR
Basingstoke and Oxford
Associated companies throughout the world
www.panmacmillan.com

ISBN 978-1-4472-0703-0

9 8 7 6 5 4 3 2 1

A CIP catalogue record for this book is available from
the British Library.

Printed and bound by CPI Group (UK) Ltd, Croydon CR0 4YY

Visit **www.picador.com** to read more about all our books
and to buy them. You will also find features, author interviews and
news of any author events, and you can sign up for e-newsletters
so that you're always first to hear about our new releases.

This book is for Mai Lin

Like a bitten apple the window
darkens slowly, the table drifts
like smoke and in the violet's grain
the weightless early dusk unfolds

ACKNOWLEDGEMENTS

Many thanks to the editors of the following books
and journals where some of these poems first appeared:
Australian Poetry Journal, Cycle Lifestyle, the *Edinburgh
Review, Identity Parade* (Bloodaxe), *The Lavender Room,
Poetry London, Poetry Review, Magma, Manhattan Review,
The Ropes* (Diamond Twig), *13 Pages*.

'An Empty House' reproduces and reconfigures a phrase
from Tom Paulin's book *The Secret Life of Poems:
A Poetry Primer* (Faber & Faber, 2008).

'Renaissance' adapts a section of Bill Berkson's essay
'What Piero Knew', from his book *The Sweet Singer
of Modernism & Other Art Writings* (Providence:
Qua Books, 2004). Many thanks are due to the author
for permission to take this liberty with his words.

Contents

Doll's House   3

Hide and Seek   4

First Bike   6

Apples and Pears   7

The Dark   8

Marsh   10

On the Move at First Light   11

Livings   12

An Empty House   13

The Ruin   14

Poem   16

Manifesto for the Makeshift   17

Following the River   18

Tarn   20

Hedge Rose   21

Keepers   22

Unearthing   24

Dark Moon   25

Lunarian   26

A Book of Water   28

The Havocs   29

Sunspot   33

Renaissance   34

Eviction   35

Two Skeletons   36

Vacancy Chain   37

The News   38

Spike   39

Virus   40

November   42

Winterbourne   43

It Will Snow Before Long   44

The Tree   46

Gloves   47

The Weasel   48

The Kick   50

Potsherds   52

The Work   54

Tribute   55

Langley Lane   56

The Bridge   59

Midnight Show   60

Last Night   61

A Room Upstairs   62

The Havocs

Doll's House

A table set with tiny plates,
the chairs around a paper fire:
diminishment has simplified
the aims and objects of desire,
while blinder faith must still provide
the mincemeat in the wooden cakes,

the creaking stair and wind outside.
For you have held your breath to peer
along the shelves of depthless books
lining a room where nothing's read;
and now, effortlessly giant, look
up to the eaves and in at the beds.

Be brave. To live is not to fear
despite the scale of what's at stake.
Two children lie in matchbox cribs.
Next door a couple, stiff as pegs,
are tucked together, rib to rib,
the bedsheets bound around their legs.

What happens if you turn away?
Every god has asked the same,
crouched at a sideboard, just in case
sudden little laughter shakes
a heaven like an empty house
where not a plate nor day will break.

Hide and Seek

I wasn't in the chicken coop,
watching. I didn't put my head
through the frayed and dusty loop
slung from the rafter in the pig shed.
I wasn't in the warm brown egg.
I wasn't in the barrel of rain
or in Grandma Dolly's beige plastic leg.
I wasn't in the rookery. I wasn't in the lanes
that powdered the cow-parsleyed hedgerows
those year-long late-summer afternoons.
I wasn't planted. I didn't grow
or constellate. I wasn't field-mushrooms,
milk or mould. I wasn't in the rabbit hole
or under the cowpat. I didn't hang
from the fence with six brother moles.
I didn't do what scarecrows can.
I didn't bark or howl or hoot.
That wasn't me in the frogspawn.
I wasn't brought in on my father's boot.
I wouldn't move like that through a field of corn.
I wasn't under my parents' bed,
listening. I wasn't in the earth
with the bones and broken crockery.
I wasn't in the cold brown Firth
with the flounders. I wasn't Lockerbie,
Annan or Langholm. I wasn't the South
or the North. I didn't wet the bed.

I wasn't in the snapdragon's mouth
or under the heap of severed heads
or under the heap of turnip heads.
I didn't rust. I wasn't waterproof
or catching. I didn't spread.
I wasn't sunburn or the truth.
I wasn't in the slurry pit.
I wasn't the accordion of baled hay
that drew breath when the string was cut.
I wasn't what I didn't say.
I wasn't the echo of the trout
ringing silently through the slow-
flowing bronze. I didn't shout
and stamp. I wasn't under the snow
that kept me from school. I wasn't slammed.
I didn't leak or scratch or smell.
I didn't go to pieces in a stranger's hands.
That wasn't my voice coming from down the well.

First Bike

There, at the bottom of the river.
Time slips. The leaves are the leaves
of woods long felled, gold still, like treasure.
The current turns one wheel as if

you had just laid it down to run
from year to year, from bright to shade,
across the bridge from being young
to here where you stand, unwise and afraid

in grown-up shoes. Your father's hand
once steadied you. When he let go
you rode, because you didn't know;

you rode across the yard to find
your balance always was your own.
You rode on after dark alone.

Apples and Pears

Hush. Sleep. Get bigger; grow older.
The world is smaller, the cold sea colder,
deader, deeper. Torchlight in the bat-cave,
lamplight on the hillside, and soon we must leave
this room in the roof, but not yet.

Quiet. Lights out. The geese go over.
Will we be rich or faithful or clever?
Our mothers' hands, like music, rest
and all the windows fill with frost.
Our fathers stand on the bottom step,
listening. Soon we must leave, but not yet.

Tuck up. Drop off. Tomorrow
is fit for us, and full of old smoke.
Time in the clock's hands, down in the duvet,
bark on the elm tree, and we've yet to go grey.
Mind in the dark, mice in the roof.
We dream the dream we each deserve.
The steep empty staircase falls away.

The Dark

When it gets too late, I have to take them out.
I cup my left hand under my right eye and with the index
finger of my right hand hold the corner of my right eye
and blink. The disc pops out. Then I blind the left.

I don't find it hard to sleep. I like the dark.
This was not the case thirty years ago
when I lay in that room in the roof and
shadows unfurled and fell from the beams.

I once made a note of something Alan Shepard said –
he was the second man to go into space, after
Yuri Gagarin. But the note is lost and the words
that might have consoled me forgotten.

Every evening we'd leave it so long night would have fallen
by the time my brother and I went down the path,
the empty hods in our hands and a black torch between us.
We'd scrape open the coal-shed door where the dark lay glittering.

This was Ted's, my grandmother wrote in her
sickbed scrawl, the note folded into the flip-top box
where my grandfather's gold engagement ring
was slotted. I thought then she was giving up.

I have a photographic memory, passed down to me
from my father, who was a master forger
of Dutch still lifes. The smells of linseed oil and noxious pigments
seethed through the kitchens of my childhood.

I do not have a photographic memory. My father,
who was not a master forger, does –
though he insists it no longer works as it did, committing
unbidden to his mind so many words without their meanings.

'Night terrors' they're called – when I woke
with my eyes open, but the dream
still happening to the walls and the doorway,
to the face of the man who called himself my father.

There's no going back. Though tonight
the moon is as close as it gets. It stares
down with its coalface of empty sockets,
its faceful of dark and speechlessness.

Marsh

where the estuary thinks
the same things as the sky;

where cows appear cloudy
and go down to the sunset to drink.

On the Move at First Light

Empty morning and the rain lies,
filling the bare field with broken panes
of pink. To loosen, to empty!
To be as full of sky as fallen rain.

Livings

I am a wielder of water. No one invites me, but I walk
through many strangers' rooms, made strange by what I've fought.

*

With a tool of metal, wood and string
I make what moves but can't be seen.

*

I am one whose livid face attests to making right.
Out of great heat I deliver what's cool and clear and bright.

*

I am one who is many. My work is play.
I'll die many times before I decay.

An Empty House

after Tom Paulin

In poetry, an empty house is always ominous.
Is an empty house in poetry always ominous?
In an empty house, poetry is always ominous.
Empty in poetry is always an ominous house.
An empty house is always in ominous poetry.
Always is an empty house, ominous in poetry.
Always is an empty house, ominous in poetry.
Always is an empty house, ominous in poetry.

The Ruin

after the Anglo-Saxon

What walls and gables, wonders still of workmanship.
Whoever's stronghold this was, havoc's jumbled it
beyond all mending, uprooting towers, rusting together tools.
What was built by strange smiths, skilled in stone,
is burst, underdug, eaten down by age: weird bricks
litter this wasteground. And what of the wrights
and hammer-men, the mortar-mixers and heavers
of slab? A long time laid off, fast in the earth,
while their sons passed, and the sons of their sons
knew no like work. But these walls withstood
mosses and snows, the fall of kings, peace's
indifferent wear by rain and rubbing kine.
Magogs raised them. Their wit matched their might.
Their great halls gawped. Their tile floors gleamed
with muscle girls and monster fish. Here
springs were housed, and happiness found haven
among men making merry, their shadows merging,
nimble as a change of mind, massive on the inner walls.

What happened? Ruin already had root. Plague came, within
and without. No one, however high, whatever wit,
was spared. Here, wide open to the wind, is where
breath was fought for, where men raved. Now birdsong
embroiders space among the rubble of what stood.
And the builders are broken down, bone by bone,
mindless and muddled together in the bottomless muck.
Half-recalled by these grim, rain-collecting courts,
by this unshattered span of arch, this blush of broken slate,
are those who twisted gold, empearled pins and gazed
on heaps of gems that beat and sparked. Houses were here.
Hot water sprang from wells and the walls held
vaults of steam and banked beds of embers, like precious stones.
Frost could get no grip. But all such days are gone.

Poem

Invisible
as air
until
a breath
lifts
and makes
palpable
the slyness
of this
snare's
devising.
Strung
in neither
window-
frame nor
ceiling
corner
but here
across
the mouth
this silver
will
hold as
long as the
weaver
of such
brief
lucidities
lurks
beneath
the tongue.

Manifesto for the Makeshift

What we lack in intelligence, we make up for
with looking. This morning, a feather at our feet,
brown-gold, tigered, toothed like a handsaw
and eyed like newly opened wood: an owl's
perhaps, snapped off to stare up from the doorstep.
We wouldn't give this feather for a ton of your technique,
and the right way to read this out loud is with growls
at the ends of the lines, and at the beginnings. Don't stop.
Not crossings but growlings-out. What we lack
in revisionary patience we make up for in volume.
This mourning for all we can't take back
deepens every day, like undergrowth's gloom
at home-time, when the song of the blackbird
is the last liquidity on earth.

Following the River

Mist had dressed the sun
like a wound when I came upon
the figure of water standing
in the naked shape of neither
man nor woman but trickling
and lapping between the two.
Its back was turned but I could see,
as if through running water, deep
into the stiller glass of it
where years swept downstream,
turning brown fields green
and then gold, piling domes
like great clouds and like the wind
undoing them. I saw engines
roll and market places
swarm and empty, the crates
and ribbed containers lifting
like sediment from the beds
of wharves and harbours;
saw faces, too, rubbed
and blurred like many coins,
catch brief light; saw
granaries filled, ships built,
laws made and maintained
across great seas and deserts
the same; and I wondered
what matter bread or justice,

maps or sweet-peas,
in the presence of one who
walks between waking,
through water's silver door?
And I saw the river,
long after stone had fallen
from stone, long after desire
and knack were barest bone,
those of kings and milkmaids,
fitters, philosophers,
butchers and cooks;
saw it flexing in moonlight,
a lens through which the moon herself
inspected her airless empery.
And I drew closer
to that streaming form
within whose live translucence
swam capitals that shivered
like fields of grey corn;
and I reached out my right hand
and my right hand was washed
and now upon my right hand
I wear like a silver glove
the acid-scald of mortal impudence.

Tarn

A star-cold dark and silence over
which you hold your face
to look as many lovely others
looked and left no trace

Hedge Rose

That seeing might embrace
the rose-alighting sky
and sun-encircling rose;
and eye undo the eye.

Keepers

The leaves fell; the potholes swilled with rain; the rain grew
oily skins of ice; the ice was smashed
and cast again in lumpy half-translucencies;
and then the holes were dry, snowdrops appeared,
the river seemed to clarify
and wobbled like a light-filled jelly as we walked;
and those six squat humdrum boxes stood.

What is it we need? Water, food and shelter; love;
to feel ourselves accreting a spoil
of enriching, meagre words to describe
one corner of an old car park, incensed
with crackling weeds, where we watched a moon couple move
from box to box, raising the combs like golden books
while the smoke-enfeebled fighters droned.

All summer I'd been reading about Saint Ambrose,
how he lay in his crib while the bees danced
over his lips, conferring eloquence. Slipping
from book to dusty book, I'd wondered when he spoke
if goodness had lit like honey his every cell.

They were draped, head to foot, in white, with helmets on,
sexless and awesome, like post-industrial seraphim.
They could have been us, attending at last to something
of substance, with a taste and use, obvious to anyone.
But we were who we were and turned from the hexagons
of fence wire we'd been peering through
to walk back along the river by the potholed footpath
the wildflowers had cracked as they sprang up,
past the ruined paper mill and into town.

Unearthing

The early autumn moon
more brightly lit and fuller grown
exposes this blue afternoon
　　an elegance of bone

Dark Moon

My last quarter was rind,
my last half, a slice of light.
The last time I was full I climbed
through the day. I was bright.

But even then, when I worked,
I hung, my own VACANCY sign;
a nothing lit up like a something:
winds without air, seas without brine.

Now I wear the hood of night
I'm disappeared, my face put out.
But I'm still here; I haven't stopped.
I can't be seen so can't be lost.

Lunarian

There's a man in you, his face like melted tallow,
for yours are the old words and yours the old
unusable, soot-grimed things. I spy you tonight,
one night from full, through a pair of cheap binoculars,
hauling up the mountainside your gong of chalk.
If there were a pond nearby upon whose surface
you might lean your subtle silver highness,
I would try to gaff and grapple you, out of courtesy,
for some nights there's more bulge to the seas,
more reflectance from your coal-bright craterscape.
But tonight unreason separates from reason,
as oil from water, dark from light, bedspread
from blackout cloth, your reflection from yourself,
O creamy, scraped-out shell of a king crab caught
off a north-east sea-coal beach, no less a beach
for glittering black, its anthracitic curve laid
down along the length of my occluded early mind
at grandpa's house in Newbiggin where at night
I heard the harbour bell clonk like a bell around
a black goat's neck. O caprine sea! O grandpa dark!
There's a moonlight man with cords of silk who binds
the destined together, but tonight my mind's
undone, great turner-away, O whole of holes,
walnut of night! You turn the tides, so give me blisters,
burn my retinas, break my heart; prove by silence
that the mouth that speaks the moon should whisper.

The night is still. The stars are fixed.
You are the moon, your silver dress,
your disappearing constancy.
The night is still. The stars are fixed:
we move through phases of the flesh.

A Book of Water

I bought a book of water,
its covers bound in weed,
its spine of muscled silver,
its words too quick to read.

I bought a book of water
I wouldn't buy again,
its one page read disorder
in letters tall as rain.

The Havocs

In the making of havoc there's me.
They carry out a post-mortem but havoc tickles the corpse and
bursts the big stitches.
Havoc is the joke the dead tell from the ground.
The living weep havoc and are told to *shhhhh*.
There is no scale of havoc.
Unlike money, havoc's never spent.
Unlike perfume, havoc has no scent.
Unlike streets of open sewers, havoc has no scent.
I am writing havoc by hand, over several nights, on watermarked
sheets of costly paper, before addressing an envelope, licking
a stamp, and walking at midnight to the post box. Sent.

I had havoc once but didn't know how to use it.
Surely there's an Index into which the havocs are entered,
because every volume I ever borrowed from the library was
missing its nouns.
Havoc pinned to the corkboard, made a note of in the margin,
filed under BUDGET, replied to, enquired about, and
finally made to stand for all the labelled, latch-able,
meshed and moulded, gleamy-as-a-boiled-sweetie
paraphernalia of organisation.
I've added havoc to my portfolio.
I want a pledge that weekly collections of havoc will be reinstated,
because of the rats and the smell.
There are no libraries left to which havoc can be returned.
There are no nouns left that are not subject to havoc.

This is the verse of havoc when the night recedes to a shade
   of lyrical blue, the moon pales, and memory is released like
      a scent from the oblivious ground.

I'm overdue myself and havoc is beating at the door to
   repossess me.
Havoc is my bonus,
Havoc my undercoat,
Havoc my open fire and havoc the sticks of furniture I will soon
   have no choice but to feed it.
When we made havoc, did the plates shift and a great wave rise
   miles out to sea?
Like a scent from the oblivious ground, the dead will rise at
   havoc's coming.
Like the scent of the dead, rising from the oblivious ground,
   havoc's coming.

Wearing havoc's hood, I launched myself as a lone crusader
   with a cape and a sentimentally manipulative backstory.
Who says havoc is a vice of the young?
As if I was a pencil and havoc went through me like the lead.
Havoc is finding it increasingly awkward to cut its own toenails.
As if I was a pencil and havoc sharpened me.
Havoc is committed to care for the elderly, education for all,
   and narrowing the gap between rich and fabulously rich.
As if I was a library and havoc closed me.
I teach havoc but no one will shut up, sit still and listen.
I supply havoc to regimes that must be able to defend
   themselves against outbreaks of peace, equality and
      artistic accomplishment.

I havoc quietly at home, where it's no one's business but my own.
If we were organized, havoc would swiftly cave in to all our
    demands.
Before it begins havoc requires, for its full effect, that you put
    these on.

The cape makes it difficult for those whom I surprise committing
    animal acts in midnight alleyways, among the wheelie bins,
        to take my havoc seriously.
More a lifestyle havoc than a necessity.
Because of the rats and the smell, a small business loan enabled me
    to start my own company, offering power washing of the
        council's havoc receptacles.
Because of the rats and the smell, a small riot enabled me to start
    my own havoc, offering random overturning, throwing and
        firing of the council's opportunity receptacles.
More a cosy havoc than a havoc that challenges the status quo
    through its refusal to make sense of anything, which is
        havoc's gift to the special few who want none of it.
More a clown in a havoc suit.

Havoc in a bottle.
Havoc in the cells.
Havoc in the cattle.
Havoc's burning smell.

Change will not happen by havoc alone.
Who said I wanted anything to change? I'm happily behavoc-ed.
As if I was a pencil and havoc kept me behind its ear.
As if I was a language and havoc spoke me.

We're thinking about getting a havoc, but we know it's a big
   responsibility.
More rats and smells, light and air, boiled sweets and libraries
   – by the havoc of all that's holy!
Shhhhh – you'll wake the change! There'll be havoc to pay.

Sunspot

Cloudless chance has let it hang for half an hour inside,
a shivering whose radiance goes undenied
by the frail billowed weave it's passing through.
The walls it doesn't touch are only dimly true.

Renaissance

after Bill Berkson

Cracklings and abrasions; cracked boards
and wormhole hollowings; scalings off,
oxidizings – greens gone to brown
or black – chemical shifts; in- and over-
painting, structural interpolations
and deletions by restorers
and less-scrupulous antiquaries: whole
works have been destroyed and parts
of panel paintings hacked away.
Rare the item that's escaped abuse:
at Arezzo, the Magdalene fresco
appears superbly intact until
one notes the large disfiguring splotch
thanks to splashings from the font.

Eviction

(Masaccio)

Barefoot, they've entered the outermost place.
She covers her breasts. He hides his face.
Behind them stands the light-filled grey stone arched
city doorway. The unworked earth is parched.
Their shadows lag and elongate,
longing towards the shade. Everything waits
to be suffered, as now the garden's streams
and orchards lie outside their lives, in dreams.

He howls into his hands. Her upturned forehead's
smooth and white; her small mouth's tearing wide.
They are after all only adequate,
and flesh, and grieve at the easily understood
threshold of grief. From where one, fully dressed
and armed, shoos them indifferently into the west.

Two Skeletons

The earth took what was offered
and now gives back our naked grins,
canine by incisor. Whose heart
quickens at our clutter? Who squats
to sweep our faceless faces clean?
The night is mine without measure.
He held me and has yet to stop.

See what's kept a little longer
than lust or fear? These ivory pots
of thoughtlessness, fallen in.
I came to pass and passed.
She was my fruit and my fire.
We lay for a while, and lie still.
Dirt made of us this diagram, desire.

Vacancy Chain

Unlike the hermit crab, no mind
can leave its outlived shape behind;
though every skull's constrained with bone
a thought not certainly its own.

The News

The rooks don't care. They wheel and croak.
The hills don't shake and turn to smoke.
The bank still doesn't give a toss
nor marble blacken in the quarry.
The cats won't don small mourning coats
and one by one come purring, *sorry*.

The trout will not refuse the fly;
the rain won't stop while you pass by
or bridges halt halfway across;
the heat won't go out of the curry
or river close its cloud-filled eye
and bow its head and murmur, *sorry*.

You want the trains to moan in tunnels,
black silk to tie the sticks in bundles,
despair to sour all candyfloss
and every brief and judge and jury
to reconvene with long lit candles
and change the law to make it sorry.

Crops will fail and crude oil spill,
but your whole grief won't even fill
your pillows, shoes or spoons with loss.
The moon's not sad; the sun won't worry.
Despite your suffering, England's still
and only some of us are sorry.

Spike

From the wood, a winter fruit
    with pips of air inside,
its core like light, like light slowed down;
    like nothing, crystallised;

fetched from the dark like light itself,
    like light itself grown old:
we touch what can't survive our touch
    but scalds our hands to hold.

Virus

Of course, we all had heinous emissions
for weeks, and for a few days even glory
was emitted heinously by the gold
in galleries where the heinous plunder
we coveted hung, or by small letters
in big books we felt too heinously
short-lived to waste our eyes upon. And then
it was summer and we got brassy
and careless, passing vulpine between us:
his vulpine scent, her tongue sliding vulpinely
over her lips; vulpine, the rooting in bins
by the heinous poor in their zip-up fox pelts,
the vulpine-red tips of the cigarettes they'd re-rolled
from the half-smoked and stubbed-out butts of our own
glowing in the vulpecular late evening gloom.

Caressed awake at weekends, we kept catching
from each other or the TV monstrous
new verbals. Someone caressed shut the front door
so hard the plunder on the wall dropped a right-angle
like a flirt. The lights came on earlier. Overseas
there was high-yield caressing to be done. Then one of us
caressed the road headfirst over the handlebars
of a racing bike and was a long time being retouched
in an antiseptic caressing house. Heinous
struck again for the way an unscarred face
could come back so different; but soon it was
gerbil for tea-towel or horsemeat for colander

after we'd all contracted the same damage
to the temporal lobe, which has lasted
until this autumn of heinous emissions: downpours
and uprisings. Heinous, what's happening in the world
and how softly we're caressed by it, but we've begun
to see more of the moon, its vulpine bib-
flash in the city dark, where we sport hats
with pointy ears and gloves with claws. Out here
we breathe easier now we can see what we say
in smoke, and all feel less gerbil.

November

You walk to the Spar for kindling
and coal, the moonlight
still locked in next door's frozen car.

Winterbourne

The red-cold sandstone doorstep glows,
you breathe blue knives, the moon's like snow
and stamped into the cast-iron lanes
are brown dead leaves with silver veins.
White fields lead down between white trees
to a frost-fired brink of glassy reeds
where light-enthralling silence lies
in one broad pane of dusty ice.

And standing on the lucid floor
you find beneath a face like yours
obliged to look from world to world
now the estranging water's stalled.
He stares and mouths. You start to speak.
The river-lid begins to creak.

It Will Snow Before Long

after Francis Jammes

It will snow before long. I remember
last year, grouching beside the fire.
When you asked me what was wrong I said:
'I want to stay here, beside the fire,
peeling oranges and toasting white bread.'

Last year in my room, while the snow
fell heavily on the fields beyond the house,
I thought hard, and with as little purpose
as the falling of the snow upon the house.
I smoked the pipe with the amber mouthpiece,

this pipe I'm smoking now; and that smell,
the smell of the houses of my childhood,
still seethes from the cupboard of dark wood
whose hinges creak as they did in my childhood.
Last year I was foolish to think that my words

were sweeter than the snow-creak of friends' footsteps.
Has nothing changed? The snow is silent
as it was when it fell last December,
and each star glitters with a snowflake's silence.
If you ask me, I'll try to remember

what was bothering me last year: the fields
beyond the house were filling up with snow
when I opened wide the cupboard of my childhood
and out spilled my childhood, like light on snow,
smelling of orange-peel and firewood.

The Tree

Tomorrow, gold and silver eggs,
the crowning star. Tonight what stands
propped up downstairs, utterly bare,
is a thrilled shade from England's
creaking, uncut, immemorial wood.

We lie awake and wonder what it means
to remember what was never there:
outlaw, fairy, white hart, winter queen;
pathless acres, dense with likelihood.

I dream we leave the lights unplugged
and let the tree be tree, fierce tree
of dark, irrefutable forest green;
that out of our baubles bright birds
hatch and sing unbroken words.

Gloves

Creaturely and soft, they lie together.
I was rude to so suddenly
open the drawer and have them stop
tickling themselves and the dark.
We make the world no better
by putting it to use, and here
your empty hands, hands of air that smell
of oil of sweat, have for years had none.

Today I took them out and tried them on.
My hands were too small, my fingers
leaving room my fingers will not fill.
A loose glove profits no man's hand.
Once I put my hand in yours, hand of my hand,
hand whose holding bettered me, and then let go.

The Weasel

That's the way the money goes . . . Trad.

Up and down the London Road
blinder by the hour
   I spent as much
   again as we owed
white winter flowers

Crowds and crowds like fallen leaves
blown between the towers
   you came in
   with the cold up your sleeves
white winter flowers

Screams and shouts and broken things
now you're fired and cower
   under the sheets
   when the postman brings
white winter flowers

Who'd have dreamt a little twist
could turn your sweet breath sour
   I tasted this
   when we first kissed
white winter flowers

For your whole heart is half my heart
my heart is half of yours
    so we're neither complete
    and lie drunk in the street
white winter flowers

The Kick

Try to and you cannot
home me here
in the long land
of new furrows
where I hunker, squat
and sleeken, all
haunch, with ears
stowed.

I could be earth
itself, but I am not
and nor do I know
any way
into or beneath it.
I sit
days out, be they
rainbowed,

thunderstruck,
bald or wisped;
and come the dusk
I lollop to crop
and work the green
corn shoots, clover
and the dew-clean
dandelion leaves.

I lie. I did not
want to move but
started I
opened air
between us.
For there is in me
such unbelonging that
given you as small excuse

I kick the world away.

Potsherds

Dug into the floors
of our houses
beneath the sea

our jars now hold
no whisper
of the cornfield

and only by their
handles can
the shapes and functions

of our ewers
be conjectured
though the evidence

of intact smaller pots
fashioned for salt
or precious spice

to weigh so sweetly
in one hand
makes clear we

variously contained
as oils and alcohols
the desiccations

of fish and flower
and in suspensions
of brine and animal fat

only those parts
of the world whose keeping
required of us an art.

The Work

for Rebecca Morales

By a lamp whose archangel's face
hangs over the earth, you search
for the unmade gesture's secret trace.

The city fills with empty light,
the paper with the livid grime
on which the zealous risk their sight.

You like the work. I like it too.
The desert's engine, silence, roars;
the night sky's fired from green to blue

but your whole mind is in your hand,
and how it moves and what it leaves
is world enough to understand.

Who knows the work, its tacky gleam,
the grit it sows behind the eyes,
the sleep it grants one tired of dreams?

Tribute

Too big now to do anything about,
our ignorance, like a season, demands
whatever we can't hold in our own two hands
in tribute: the wind; snowflakes; the shadow of a doubt.
We tried what we thought had to be tried,
imposing barrows and ditches, grasses and rules;
feeding our crumpled gold to black implacable pools;
and still we wonder why the weather died.

We're in the open of our unknowing,
unsuitably dressed, shaking the standard of a blown-
inside-out umbrella as the rain pours
skywards and the great airstreams stop flowing.
For a time at least our hands were our own
and absently we shut with them our brilliant doors.

Langley Lane

Stand up straight, my son. Don't slouch.
  Mother, I'm not slouching.
There's nothing you need hide from me.
  You know I don't like touching.

A mother must – it's in my hands
  to touch what's mine so briefly,
to touch my son for one small proof
  that he's still strong and loves me.

*Mother, I wish you weren't at home
  and I could sit in peace.
I'd hoped to meet the dark alone
  and not to cause a fuss.*

My son, I'm bound to love no less
  the child who brings me pain.
My son, what spreads across your shirt?
  You need not hide a stain.

*What I hide won't be undone
  and I'd not see your face
to spare myself the sight of one
  whose grief is my disgrace.*

Take a chair, my son, you're tired.
  Drink a glass of milk.
You're up, you're down. Your brain's still soft.
  Your adulthood half built.

You're pale, my son – you'll fade away:
    you need a bite to eat.
Once I was young and like you swayed
    unsteady on my feet –

Mother, soon I'll get my rest
    so while I can I'll stand.
My son, what's loose at your left wrist?
    What's spilling from your hand?

Mother, my hand is full of shame.
    It's pouring from my heart.
I've walked it in from Langley Lane
    where trouble's known to start.

If trouble starts, you've said to me,
    just turn and walk away.
But Langley Lane's blind corner led
    to five who blocked my way.

You're on our turf, one said, and spat.
    The youngest-looking shoved
me first; I shoved him harder back.
    He punched me in the chest.

The leaves were still. The sun came out
    to scatter coins of light
and I saw gripped in his right fist
    a little silver spike.

A spike at which I stared, surprised –
  a bloody silver spike
at which he also stared, surprised,
  our two boys' looks alike.

The sun went in. A siren moaned.
  Clouds crawled across the blue.
They grabbed my phone. I started home –
  what else was there to do?

My son, you walked from Langley Lane?
  I walked from Langley Lane.
I took small steps and often stopped
  to breathe around the pain.

My son, you walked from Langley Lane.
  I walked from Langley Lane.
I held myself to slow the stain
  and walked from Langley Lane.

The Bridge

The trees are leaking shadows
where they stand upon the hill
and as we walk the mountain throws
a slate-blue chill.

I hold her hard hand tighter
for we've turned away from home
and my apron glows like hers
in the dusty copper gloom.

Where are we going, mother?
Where we haven't been before.
The river's spent its silver.
The day's a bolted door.

You'll get back nothing tomorrow
you touched or heard or saw.
The bridge we cross is sorrow's
and this is sorrow's law.

Midnight Show

Afterwards, the fading score
and final print too small to read,
the dark like sleep, and glow that leads
back down the low-lit corridor
and staircase hung with early stars
to popcorn kettles cooling off,
the cashed-up, blacked-out ticket booth
and frosted doors you drift towards
behind two lovers, slow to leave,
who hand in hand go unaware
across the lobby, through stale air
a childhood's sweetness haunts, achieve
the night at last and briefly turn
to let you pass, a man alone
whose face, like theirs, is not his own
but flickers still with something burned
into his eyes by that long dream
of light that played upon the screen.

Last Night

At the end what we'll wish we'd done
more often was lock in our noise
and books and pocket the glimmer
of the key and then while the glow
was still leaving our eyes and heaven
remained doubtful, depthless and un-starred
walk into the live air under the trees
in dark from which an everyday hill
grew out of the world to allow
two to climb and sit as if at the mouth
of a cave and stare into the back
of sun and word, once and before
reading in the rare ordinary night
their freedom to want for nothing more

A Room Upstairs

My friends, we've had a childhood, lasted childhood's slow
days, insoluble in the rain, childhood's glow
of days that drove long into nights that would not fall
while we sat listening in the leftover heat to others call

across the fields, from dark outskirts of oak
and pine, from cardboard dens that trickled smoke,
from sources of water or knowledge or pain,
and refused, as they had, to answer to our given names.

My sons and daughters, you whom I cannot hold or hear,
whose likely names now fill my house with neither love nor fear,
whose childhood things are boxed up still, unsold, or unmade
or unthought of, whose souls remain unweighed

by hand or blame or purpose; my girls and boys,
for you the woods were set going like a frightening toy
by the shadows' clockwork, long ago, while you lay beyond
all calling home, on the far side of the drowning pond

or in the disused cattleshed, or high in the arms
of the hanging tree, and whispered my name
so clearly it carried across the summer night
and summer dawn, and autumn days, and years, like light,

until, far from the kingdom of childhood, I heard.
The stone is closed and I no longer know the word
to open the wall behind the bed. The steps don't lead
down into the ground beneath the door grown through with weeds

to chambers lit by taproot chandeliers.
I cannot knock on water and watch myself disappear,
like breath from a mirror, as an entrance of air's
unsealed midstream. My friends, there is a room upstairs

where no one is but someone moves:
we shelter the unnamed whom love's
mislaid, and it is for them that we listen on
in the quiet between the last bus and the blackbird's song.

Outer Banks, N.C.

Hot gloom and the beach like salt.
The great sea turtle lies, its belly blown open.
All night the mind had dreamed itself clean.